W9-AQC-689

Date: 9/4/12

J 508.2 OWE
Owen, Ruth,
How do you know it's fall? /

Signs of the Seasons

How Do You Know It's Fall?

by Ruth Owen

Consultants:

Suzy Gazlay, MA
Recipient, Presidential Award for Excellence in Science Teaching

Kimberly Brenneman, PhD
National Institute for Early Education Research,
Rutgers University, New Brunswick, New Jersey

BEARPORT PUBLISHING

NEW YORK, NEW YORK

Credits

Cover and Title Page, © Robert Neumann/Shutterstock, and, © Elena Elisseeva/Shutterstock, and, © Joyfull/Shutterstock; 4L, © Anat-oli/Shutterstock; 4R, © Steve Heap/Shutterstock; 5TR, © Ying/Shutterstock; 5, © doraclub/Shutterstock; 7, © Studio J Inc./Purestock/Superstock; 8L, © Monkey Business Images/Shutterstock; 8BL, © Elena Elisseeva/Shutterstock; 8BC, © Mitzy/Shutterstock; 8BR, © CoolR/Shutterstock; 9T, © Nagel Photography/Shutterstock; 9, © Kzenon/Shutterstock; 10L, © DimasEKB/Shutterstock; 11, © S. Borisov/Shutterstock; 12L, © Prisma/Superstock; 12BR, © seroymac/Shutterstock; 13, © Cusp/Superstock; 14L, © Artem Perebyinis/Shutterstock; 14BC, © Saje/Shutterstock; 15T, © Imagebroker/FLPA; 15B, © Shooarts/Shutterstock; 16L, © John Hawkins/FLPA; 17, © Michael Rose/FLPA; 18, © Glenn Young/Shutterstock; 19T, © Arto Hakola/Shutterstock; 19B, © David Hosking/FLPA; 20L, © Bochkarev Photography/Shutterstock; 21, © Blend Images/Superstock; 22TL, © Elena Elisseeva/Shutterstock; 22TR, © SAJE/Shutterstock; 22BL, © AMA/Shutterstock; 22BC, © dionisvera/Shutterstock; 22BR, © IrinaK/Shutterstock; 23TL, © LlaneM/Shutterstock; 23TC, © Inc/Shutterstock; 23TR, © CoolR/Shutterstock; 23BL, © Jose Ignacio Soto/Shutterstock; 23BC, © Johnny Lye/Shutterstock; 23BR, © Vladimir Mucibabic/Shutterstock.

Library of Congress Cataloging-in-Publication Data

Owen, Ruth, 1967–
  How do you know it's fall? / by Ruth Owen.
    p. cm. — (Signs of the seasons)
  Includes bibliographical references and index.
  ISBN-13: 978-1-61772-396-4 (library binding)
  ISBN-10: 1-61772-396-7 (library binding)
  1. Autumn—Juvenile literature. I. Title.
  QB637.7.O94 2012
  508.2—dc23
                          2011044572

For more information, write to Bearport Publishing Company, Inc., 45 West 21st Street, Suite 3B, New York, New York 10010. Printed in the United States of America in North Mankato, Minnesota.

10 9 8 7 6 5 4 3 2 1

Contents

It's Fall!

Every year has four seasons—spring, summer, fall, and winter.

As summer comes to an end, fall begins.

For many farmers, fall is **harvest** time.

They gather **crops** that they've grown, such as apples and pumpkins.

When you spot fat, orange pumpkins for sale, it's a sign that fall is here!

wheat

corn

In fall, corn, wheat, and other crops are ready to be eaten. Farmers gather the crops that they grow in fields so that people can buy them.

pumpkins

Shorter Days

In summer, each day has more hours of sunlight than darkness.

By the time fall arrives, night and day are about the same length.

Then, all through fall, daytime becomes shorter than nighttime.

Each year, fall starts on either September 22 or September 23. The first day of fall is marked on calendars.

Keep a diary that shows how daytime gets shorter in fall. Each week in fall, pick a day and draw a clock that shows what time it got dark outside.

September

Su	M	T	W	Th	F	Sa
						1
2	3	4	5	6	7	8
9	10	11	12	13	14	15
16	17	18	19	20	21	(22)
23	24	25	26	27	28	29
30						

first day of fall

How early did it get dark outside?

Date	Sunset time
Oct 1	
Oct 8	
Oct 15	

Frosty Mornings

Fewer hours of daylight are not the only clue that fall is starting.

The weather begins to feel cooler, too.

On some mornings, everything outside is covered with **frost**.

Chilly mornings, windy days, and rain can all be signs that fall is here!

a rainy day

On a chilly fall morning, go outside on a frost treasure hunt. Try to spot a flower, spider web, and leaf that are covered with frost.

If a person or animal's breath makes a little cloud when they breathe out, it's a sign that the weather is cold!

breath

frost

Crunchy Leaves

fall leaves

Sidewalks and parks covered with crunchy leaves are clues that it's fall.

As summer comes to an end, the leaves on many trees change color.

Green leaves turn red, yellow, orange, and brown.

Then the leaves fall from the branches and flutter to the ground.

The leaves that fall to the ground become food for **insects** and worms.

Become a fall leaf collector. Find as many different shapes and colors of leaves as you can. Then glue or tape them into a notebook or scrapbook.

Apple Time

All through summer, apples on trees grow bigger and fatter.

When fall arrives, the apples are ready to eat.

Farmers climb ladders to pick them.

The apples are then loaded onto trucks that go to supermarkets.

a farmer picking apples

Look at the **seeds** inside an apple. What important job do you think the seeds have?

seeds

In fall, people can visit apple farms to pick the fruit.

Time for Seeds

Fall is the season when many plant seeds fall to the ground.

Some seeds, such as those from apple trees, fall to the ground inside a piece of fruit.

Other seeds, such as the ones from maple trees, whirl to the ground like tiny helicopters.

The seeds from oak trees fall to the ground inside a tough shell called an acorn.

maple tree

maple seed

After the seeds have fallen to the ground, they wait in the soil where they landed. When the weather warms up, they will grow into new plants.

Acorns sometimes get buried underground after they have fallen from a tree. How do you think this might happen?

acorns

Getting Ready for Winter

squirrel

On a frosty fall morning, a busy squirrel collects acorns and other seeds.

It digs little holes in the ground and buries the food.

In winter, when it is hard to find enough to eat, the squirrel will dig up the food.

It won't find all the seeds it buried, however.

The ones it does not find will grow into new plants and trees!

acorn

16

a squirrel burying food

Squirrels bury the food they collect to hide it from animals such as birds, chipmunks, and other squirrels.

17

Honk! Honk! It's Fall!

One sign of fall is the "honk, honk" of Canada geese as they fly south.

Canada geese live in many parts of Canada and the United States.

As the weather gets colder in the fall, the birds fly off to warm places in the south to spend the winter.

In spring, they fly back north.

Canada goose

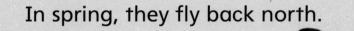

When Canada geese fly together in a group, they fly in a V shape.

A Garden in Fall

In fall, people are busy cleaning up their gardens.

They rake up leaves that fall from the trees and cut down summer flowers that have died.

They also plant flowers **bulbs**, which will grow into daffodils and other flowers in spring.

Fall is the season when people prepare their gardens for the long, cold winter.

planting bulbs

Stand outside on a fall day.
What signs of fall can you see?
What sounds do you hear?
What do you smell?

Fall lasts until December 20 or 21. Then winter begins!

raking up leaves

21

Science Lab

When you are playing in your backyard, on the playground at school, or in the park, go on a fall treasure hunt.

See how many of the things on the Fall Treasure Hunt list you can see, smell, hear, or collect.

If it's not fall where you live, then draw a picture of a fall scene.

Include as many things from the list as you can.

Then when fall comes to where you live, go outside and try to find the things you included in your drawing.

Fall Treasure Hunt

Things to see
Fruit hanging on a tree

A small animal gathering food

Seeds in a flower

Canada geese flying in a V shape

A dry, dead flower

Things to smell
Damp leaves

A frosty morning

Things to hear
Leaves crunching under your feet

A bird rustling in dry leaves

A seed falling to the ground

Things to collect
An acorn

A seed with wings

Ten leaves with different shapes and colors

Science Words

bulbs (BUHLBZ) the rounded underground parts of some plants; food for the plant is stored in the bulb

crops (KROPS) plants that are grown in large quantities on a farm

frost (FRAWST) a thin layer of ice that forms when temperatures are below freezing

harvest (HAR-vist) the picking or collecting of food crops that are ready to be eaten

insects (IN-sekts) small animals that have six legs, three main body parts, two antennas, and a hard covering called an exoskeleton

seeds (SEEDZ) small parts of a plant that can grow into a new plant

Index

Read More

Bullard, Lisa Marie. *Leaves Fall Down; Learning about Autumn Leaves.* Mankato, MN: Picture Window Books (2010)

McKneally, Ranida T. *Our Seasons.* Watertown, MA: Charlesbridge (2007).

Rustad, Martha E. H. *Fall Weather: Cooler Temperatures.* Minneapolis, MN: Millbrook Press (2011).

Learn More Online

To learn more about fall, visit **www.bearportpublishing.com/SignsoftheSeasons**

About the Author

Ruth Owen has been developing, editing, and writing children's books for more than ten years. She particularly enjoys working on books about animals and the natural world. Ruth lives in Cornwall, England, just minutes from the ocean. She loves gardening and caring for her family of llamas.